DON'T MAKE ME USE MY NURSE VOICE

ADULT COLORING BOOK FOR NURSES

Rocket Publishing

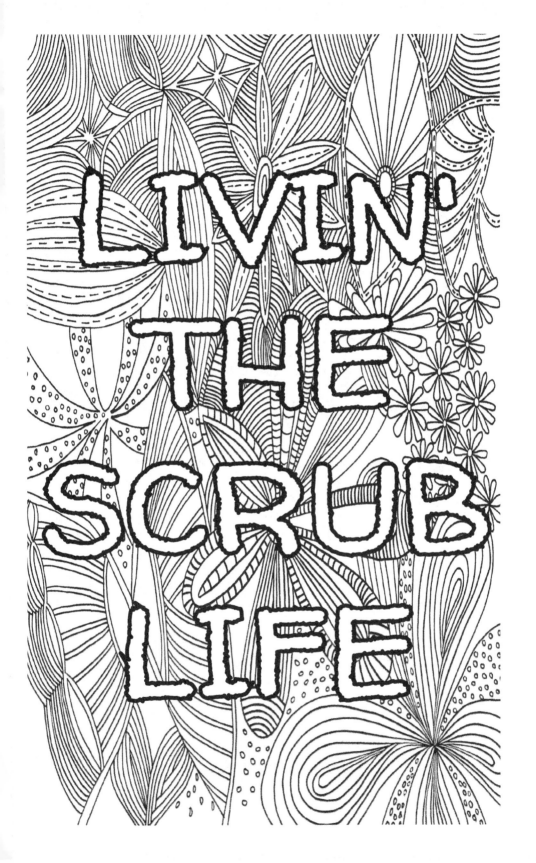

I LOVE BEING A NURSE
BUT MOST OF ALL
I JUST LOVE
WEARING SCRUBS.
THEY'RE THE CLOSEST
THING TO PAJAMAS.

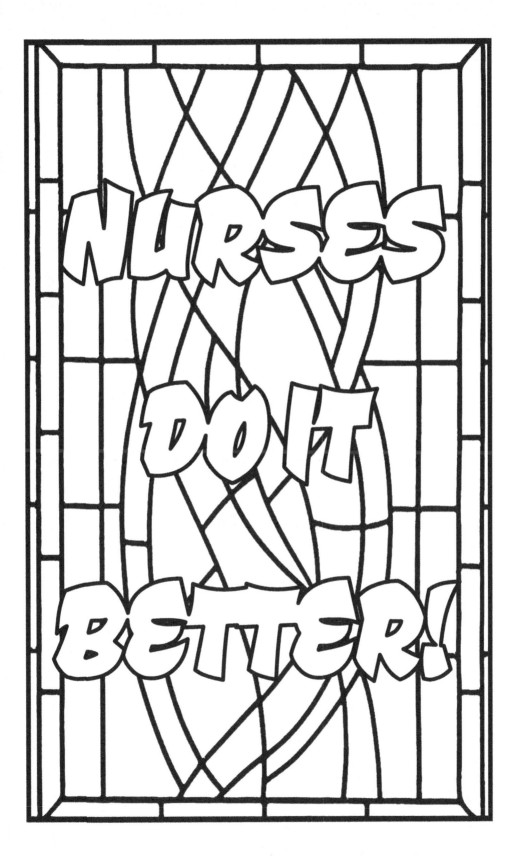

NURSES
LIKE IT
HARDER
FASTER
DEEPER
CPR SAVES LIVES

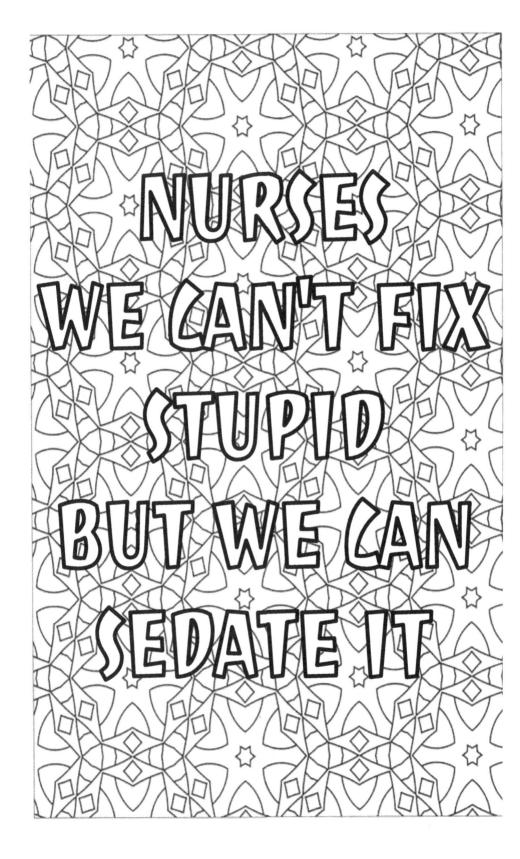

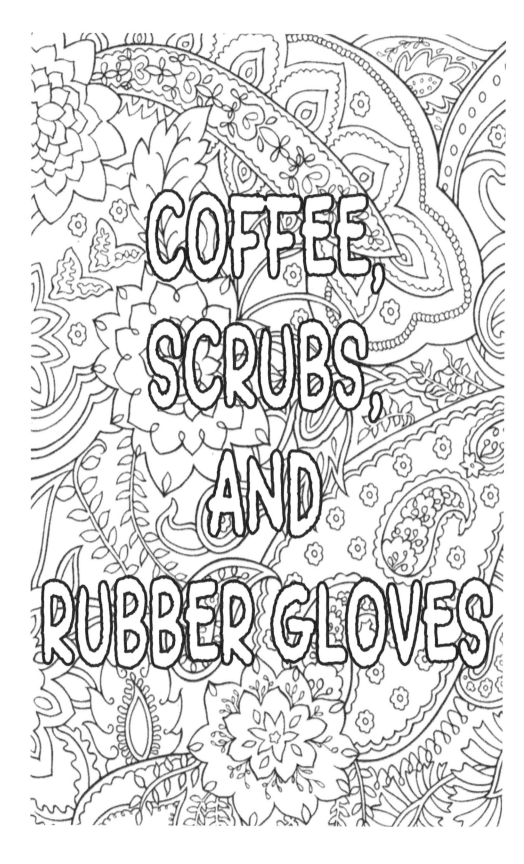

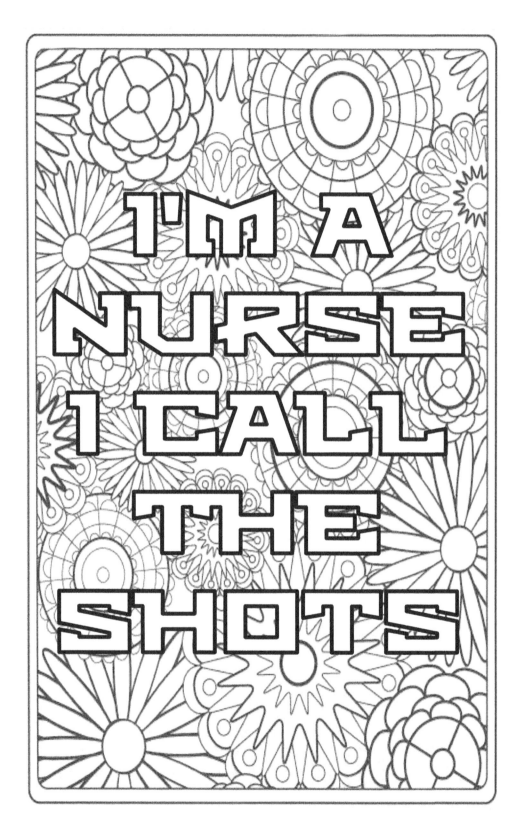

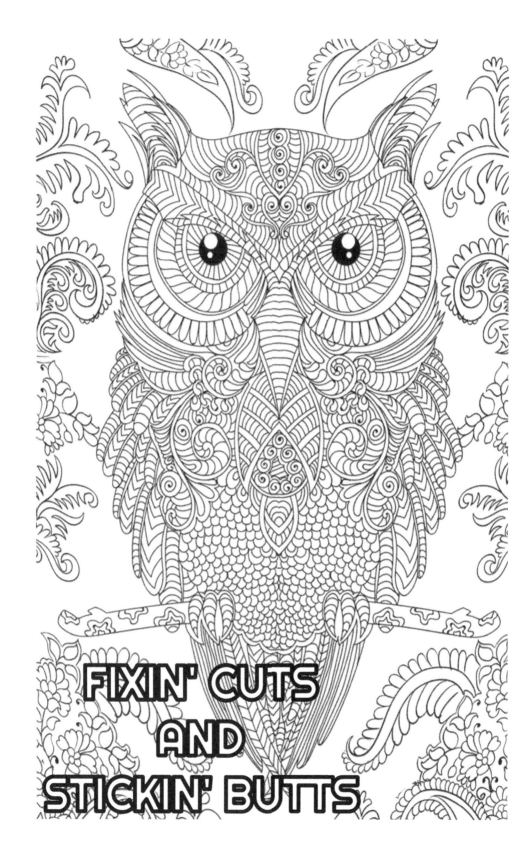

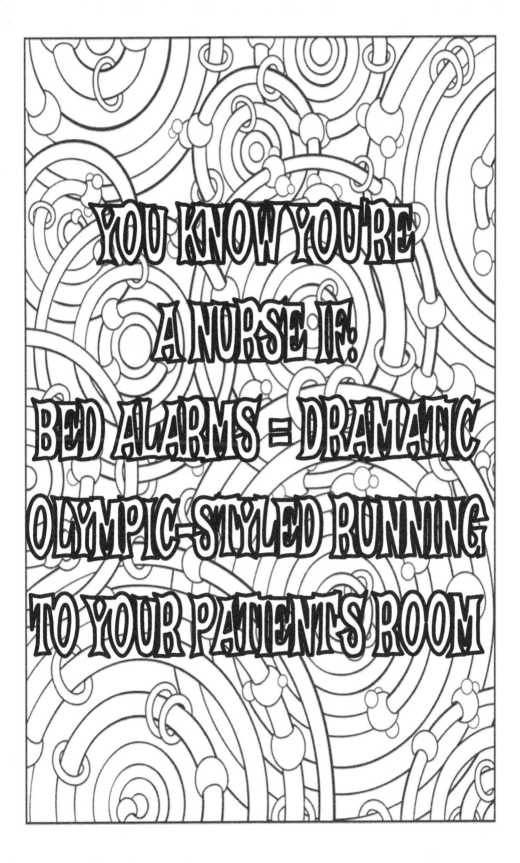

BE NICE TO NURSES: WE KEEP THE DOCTORS FROM ACCIDENTALLY KILLING YOU

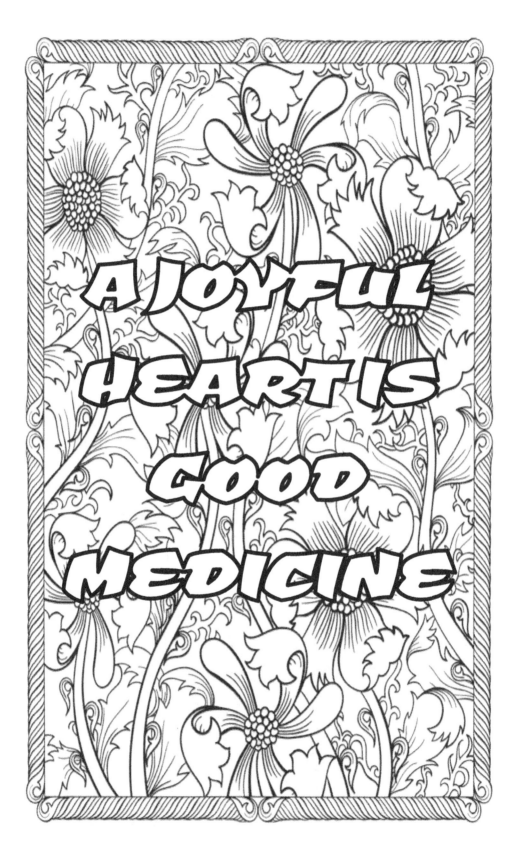

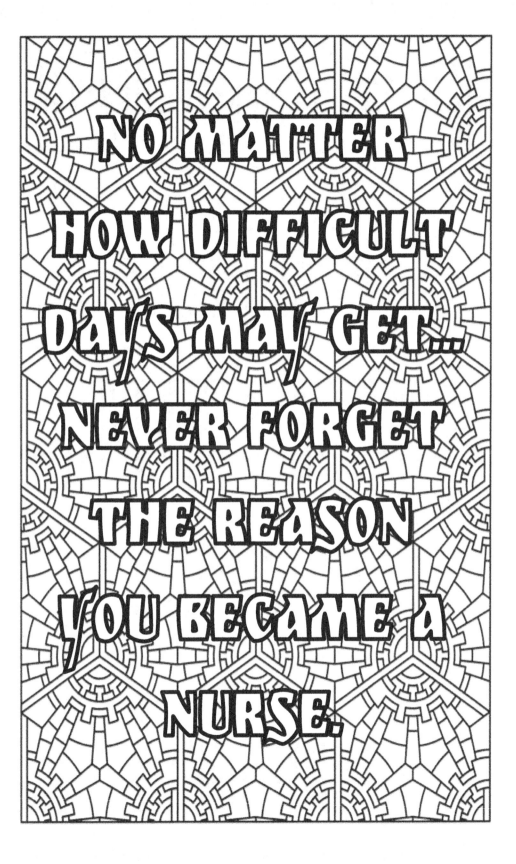

NURSE SURVIVAL: CAFFEINE BEFORE SHIFT, ALCOHOL AFTER

YOU THINK MONDAYS ARE BAD? TRY WORKING WEEKENDS, HOLIDAYS, AND 12 HOUR NIGHTS!

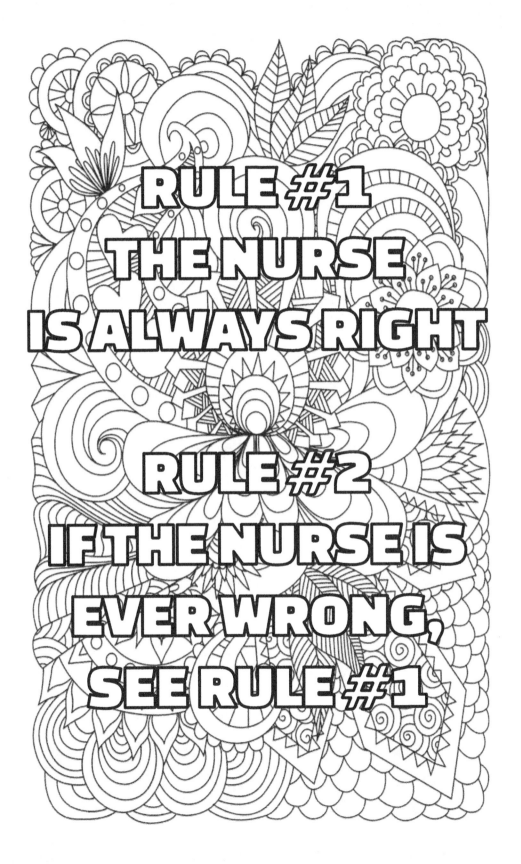

A WONDERFUL
NURSE IS
HARD TO FIND
&
IMPOSSIBLE TO
FORGET

NURSING: A PROFESSION WHERE YOU MUST ALSO WASH YOUR HANDS BEFORE USING THE RESTROOM

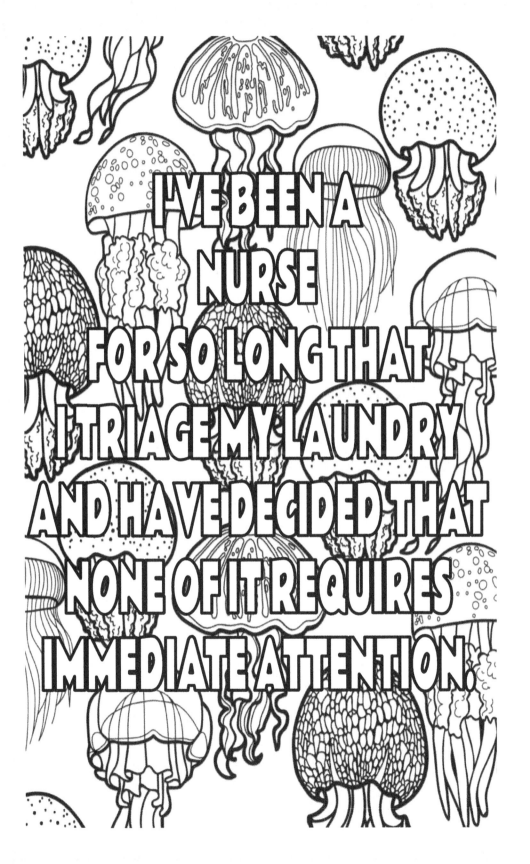

I HAVE A GREAT JOKE
ABOUT HIPAA
BUT I CAN'T TELL YOU

DON'T PISS OFF NURSES, THEY'RE LIKE THE MAFIA. PISS OFF ONE AND YOU PISS OFF THE REST.

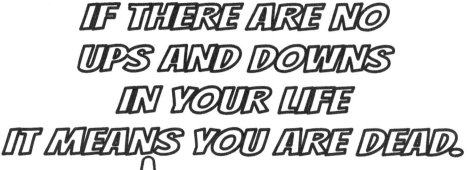

IF THERE ARE NO
UPS AND DOWNS
IN YOUR LIFE
IT MEANS YOU ARE DEAD.

I WILL STAB YOU

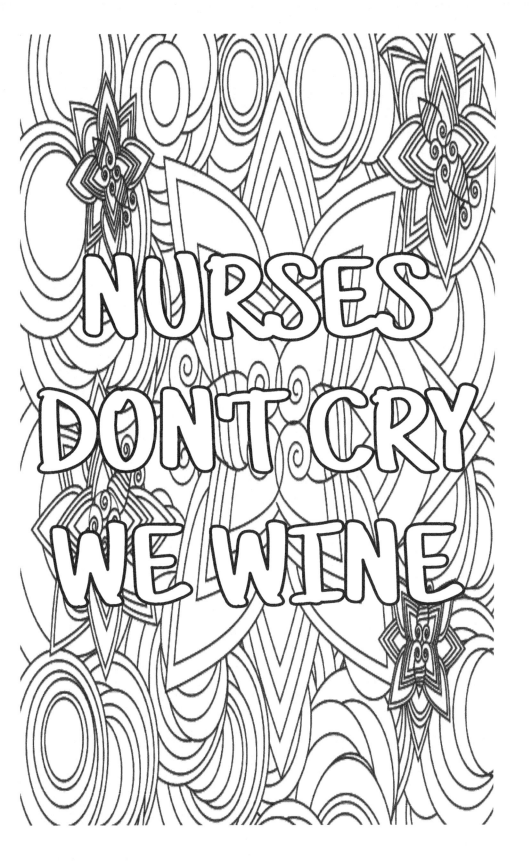

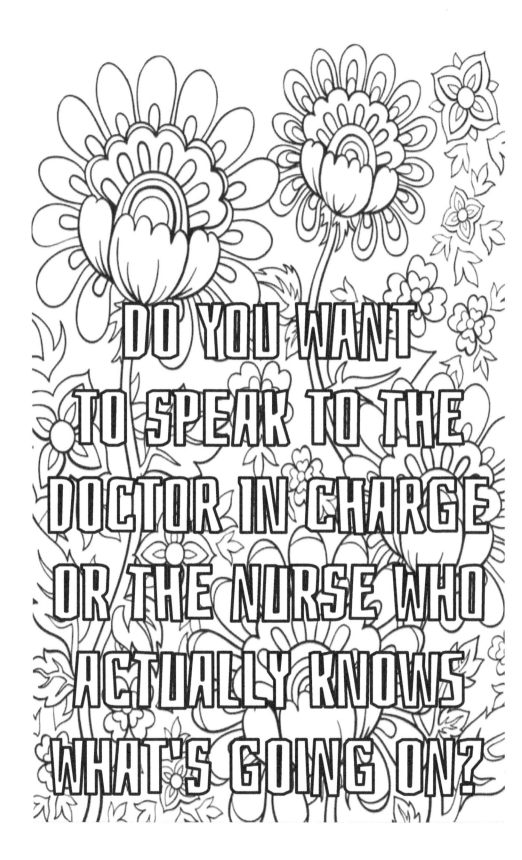

Made in the USA
Monee, IL
01 February 2022